AN INTRODUCTION TO KAMILA SHAMSIE'S *HOME FIRE*

AN INTRODUCTION TO KAMILA SHAMSIE'S *HOME FIRE*

ABBIE JUKES

Greenwich Exchange
London

Acknowledgements
For Ben, who has been with me and supported me since day one. And also for my PhD supervisor, Katie Fleming, without whom this book would not have come to fruition.

Greenwich Exchange, London

First published in Great Britain in 2023
All rights reserved

An Introduction to Kamilla Shamsie's Home Fire
© Abbie Jukes 2023

This book is sold subject to the conditions that it shall not, by way of trade or otherwise, be lent, resold, hired out or otherwise circulated without the publisher's prior consent in any form of binding or cover other than that in which it is published and without a similar condition including this condition being imposed on the subsequent purchaser.

Printed and bound by imprintdigital.com
Cover design by December Publications
Tel: 07951511275

Greenwich Exchange Website: www.greenex.co.uk

Cataloguing in Publication Data is available from the British Library

Cover: Courtesy of Shutterstock

ISBN: 978-1-910996-69-0

For all the women who continue to fight
to make their voices heard

'If people were silent, nothing would change.'
– Malala Yousafzai

CONTENTS

Introduction 13

PART I: SOPHOCLES' *ANTIGONE*

Background to Sophocles' *Antigone* 14

Antigone and Gender 17

Antigone, the Nature of the Law and the Debate Between the State and Individual 22

Antigone's Claim 24

Creon the Tyrant? 26

PART TWO: KAMILA SHAMSIE'S *HOME FIRE*

Home Fire's Relationship to *Antigone* 28

Home Fire and Gender Relations 31

The Nature of the Law in *Home Fire* 35

The Issue of Citizenship in *Home Fire* 41

Concluding Thoughts 46

Introduction

Kamila Shamsie's *Home Fire* is an adaptation of the Ancient Greek tragedy *Antigone*. Kamila Shamsie is a Pakistani and British author, born in Karachi Pakistan, 1973. Although the focus of this guide will be on *Home Fire,* Shamsie is the author of eight books, which include *Home Fire* (2017) and *Burnt Shadow* (2010). *Home Fire* won the women's prize for fiction in 2018, and as such, is arguably the most well-known of her books.

The backdrop to Kamila Shamsie's *Home Fire* is Sophocles' *Antigone*, an ancient Greek tragedy. In *Antigone*, a young girl Antigone buries her brother, Polynices against the wishes of state-ruler Creon. For doing so, Antigone is sentenced to death by her uncle who also happens to be the king of Thebes. Sophocles' *Antigone* is key to understanding the events of *Home Fire,* and the first part of the book will be dedicated to exploring this play in more detail.

Written more than two millennia after Sophocles' *Antigone*, Shamsie's *Home Fire* is set in Britain in the twenty-first century, consentrating on the lives of British Muslims. It takes place mainly in London, but also has scenes in America and Syria. The book is divided into narratives, which are all told in third person style, but also features snippets from newspapers and social media. Each character in *Home Fire* is based on characters from Sophocles'

Antigone: sisters Isma (Ismene in *Antigone*) and Aneeka (Antigone in *Antigone*) and their brother Parvaiz (Polynices in *Antigone*). Yet whilst there is a fourth sibling in *Antigone*, Eteocles, there is no fourth sibling in *Home Fire*. The other narratives in *Home Fire* are those of Home Secretary Karamat (Creon) and Karamat's son, Eamonn (Haemon). A major difference between Sophocles' *Antigone* and Kamila Shamsie's *Home Fire*, however, is that the Creon-based character Karamat does not have a familial relationship in *Home Fire*. In *Antigone*, Creon is the state-ruler of Thebes but is also uncle to Antigone, Ismene, Polynices and Eteocles.

Before going into more detail about the characters in *Home Fire*, however, we will explore Sophocles' *Antigone* in the first part of the book. Understanding Sophocles' *Antigone* is necessary to understand how Shamsie uses the plot of the ancient play in her own novel. After we have explored Sophocles' *Antigone* in detail, we will then look at how Shamsie builds on the themes that are raised in the ancient play – gender, citizenship and the nature of the law – and how they have been altered for the contemporary setting of *Home Fire*.

PART 1: SOPHOCLES' *ANTIGONE*

Background to Sophocles' *Antigone*

Arguably, no Greek tragedy holds such a privileged place in scholarship or is written about as prolifically as Sophocles' *Antigone*. Indeed, academic critic George Steiner reports that European poets, philosophers and scholars from the eighteenth to twentieth centuries considered *Antigone* 'not only the finest of Greek tragedies, but a work of art nearer to perfection than any other produced by the human spirit.'[1] This reputation continues into the present day. For instance, in October 2021 alone, at least three new Antigone plays were produced, including Kamal Kaan's *Aaliyah: After Antigone*, performed in Bradford,[2] poet Hollie McNish's adaptation of *Antigone* for Storyhouse Theatre,[3] and a gender-switching version of *Antigone*, staged at Colchester's Mercury Theatre.[4]

Written around the fifth-century BCE, (before common era) Sophocles' *Antigone* is, by contemporary convention, the final play in a 'trilogy' preceded by *Oedipus the King* and *Oedipus at Colonus*.[5] This does not necessarily mean that in the ancient world, the plays were supposed to be placed together.

---

[1] George Steiner, 'Chapter One', in *Antigones*, Oxford Paperbacks, reprint (Oxford: Oxford Univ. Press, 1986), pp1-106 (p1).

[2] Mark Fisher, '*Aaliyah: After Antigone* Review – Sophocles's Moral Dilemmas Play out in Bradford', *The Guardian*, 11 October 2021, section Stage <https://www.theguardian.com/stage/2021/oct/11/aaliyah-after-antigone-review-sophocless-impact-hub-bradford> [accessed 11 October 2021].

[3] 'Antigone', *Storyhouse* <https://www.storyhouse.com/event/antigone> [accessed 20 October 2021].

[4] Chris Wiegand, 'Antigone Review – Gender Switch Sparks Striking Take on Sophocles', *The Guardian*, 8 October 2021, section Stage <https://www.theguardian.com/stage/2021/oct/08/antigone-review-mercury-theatre-colchester> [accessed 11 October 2021].

[5] The three plays each belong to separate trilogies, the other plays of which do not survive, and hence have been grouped together to form a set. See versions of the three plays, like Penguin – the one used in this book – and Oxford, which have published them as a trilogy.

Aged just twelve or thirteen, Antigone buries her brother Polynices and in so doing defies the orders of her uncle, the state ruler, Creon. As Polynices killed their brother Eteocles, who was king at the time of his death, Polynices is deemed to be a traitor of the state and Creon orders that 'he must be left unburied, his corpse/carrion for the birds and dogs to tear'.[6] Despite Antigone's sister Ismene's pleas to obey Creon, Antigone does not listen. She is condemned to a living death – sent to a cave to be buried alive – at his hands. Antigone decides that she does not want to die in the cave, and so commits suicide by hanging herself with a rope.

Antigone is not the only victim of the tragedy, however. Death both begins and ends the play. Creon's son, Haemon – also Antigone's fiancé and cousin – kills himself in protest against Creon's edict, and Creon's wife Eurydice follows suit. Extensive scholarship – much beyond the confines of traditional classical studies – has focused on and continues to write about *Antigone*. These debates include the philosophical G.W.F. Hegel, (Oxford: Oxford University Press, 2013), to postcolonial in Tina Chanter's *Whose Antigone? The Tragic Marginalisation of Slavery* (Albany: State University of New York Press, 2011) and the feminist Fanny Söderbäck (ed), *Feminist Readings of Antigone* (Albany: State University of New York Press, 2010).

This section has introduced Sophocles' *Antigone*. We will now focus in detail on the themes that are explored in the play – gender, the nature of the law and the family versus the state. The second part of the book will explore how Kamila Shamsie's *Home Fire* builds on these in her novel.

---

[6]Sophocles, *Antigone*, II. 229-30, p68.

Antigone and Gender

The conflict between Antigone and Creon at the heart of this tragedy is amongst its most compelling elements. Central to its dramatic impact is the fact that this dispute is deliberately staged as markedly gendered: a young woman confronts and is confronted by an older man. The gendered significance of this scene, for its ancient audience, would have been obvious and immediate. Antigone's disobedience would not simply have represented political subordination but would have called into question the gender roles which each character represents, and which would have been seen to subtend the social, legal, and political organisation of the city.

Creon's fury at Antigone burying her brother is not simply because she contradicted his edict not to bury Polynices, as a traitor to the state, but also because Antigone is a woman. Her behaviour disrupts gender roles: in disobeying the law of the city, and in carrying out the forbidden burial, Antigone is said to be behaving in a 'manly' way, and additionally, threatens Creon's masculinity: 'I am not the man, not now: she is the man/if this victory goes to her and she goes free.'[7] The representation of Creon's understanding of the nature of political and legal organisation suggests that their institution was seen by the contemporary audience to be highly gendered.[8]

This gendered element also extends to the ways in which we might

---

[7] Sophocles, *Antigone*, ll. 541-42, p83.

[8] The implications of the gender politics in the play would of course change if Creon was female, as in the case of this *Antigone* play, performed in October 2021. See Chris Wiegand, 'Antigone Review – Gender Switch Sparks Striking Take on Sophocles'.

analyse the tragic components – in Aristotelian ways – of the plot. Creon's fatal flaw – or *hamartia* – Susan C. Caprio argues, is that Creon fails to understand Antigone's request to bury her brother is because he is suffering from '*hamartia* – his blindness to the strength of human love'.[9] Caprio goes on to reason exactly why Creon's apparent *hamartia* results in his fear of losing his manhood: 'Another, more specifically feminist, way of interpreting his *hamartia* is to focus on his morbid fear of emasculation in surrendering to the force of a woman's argument – even worse, his metamorphosis into one of the despised creatures should he acknowledge the validity of Antigone's defense of her action'.[10] Further supporting Caprio's reasoning, Antigone states how she 'was born to join in love, not hate – /that is my nature'.[11] Opposed to Antigone's proclamation of her loving nature, Creon responds by exclaiming, 'Go down below and love,/if love you must – love the dead!'.[12] Creon's emphasis on 'if love you must' is evidence that he believes that love is a choice, not because of familial duty, and certainly not as a result of understanding his isolated and suffering niece. Moreover, Caprio's choice to use the word 'despised' to describe Creon's attitude towards womanhood openly demonstrates that Creon's treatment of Antigone occurs because she is a woman. If Antigone were replaced with a man, it is possible that Creon would consider the pleas being made to him.

---

[9]Susan C. Caprio, 'A Feminist Approach to Classical Literature', *CEA Critic*, 48 (1985), 62-67 (p64).

[10]Caprio, p64.

[11]Sophocles, *Antigone*, l. 590, p86.

[12]Sophocles, *Antigone*, ll. 591-92, p86.

Particularly for a modern-day audience, Creon's treatment of Antigone is definitively misogynist; misogynist meaning somebody who is deeply prejudiced about women. Yet, according to Rowan Williams in *The Tragic Imagination*, Creon is not a misogynist: 'Creon is not being a primitive sexist; the point is that he will cease to be what he is if a political decision – a decision taken about the limits of the law, about who counts as existing in a law-governed city – is going to be taken by a woman'.[13] Although Williams points out that Creon is not a 'sexist', as Creon made the decision about Antigone based on the existence of a law-abiding state, Williams' remark is still inherently sexist. Williams does not comment on whether this action would be taken by Creon if a man – not a woman – were to act in the same way Antigone had.

Opposed to Williams, many critics hold the view that Creon treats Antigone as he does because Creon's behaviour is misogynistic. Omolara Kikelomo Owoeye argues that Creon's treatment of women originates 'from Creon's unconscious, revealing societal and prejudicial belief that women are to constantly remain indoors and not meddle in the affairs of State since those are the responsibilities of the men'.[14] Although, of course, other readings of Creon focus on aspects of his relationship with Antigone, arguably, even if Creon is acting in the interests of the fifth-century Athenian state, misogyny

---

[13] Rowan Williams, 'Reconciliation and its Discontents: Thinking with Hegel', in *The Tragic Imagination* (Oxford: Oxford University Press, 2016), pp56-81 (p59).

[14] Omolara Kikelomo Owoeye, 'Gender Pride as Tragic Flaw in Sophocles' *Antigone*', *Research in Gender Studies,* 2 (2012), 101-114 (p110).

still underlies his treatment of women in *Antigone* – especially Antigone herself.

One possible explanation for Creon's treatment of women is the threat that it poses to his position of power. There are several instances in Sophocles' *Antigone* where Creon expresses his fear of being 'unmanned' by the actions of Antigone. One likely reason for this behaviour is that Creon does not want to be viewed as the 'weaker' sex. Speaking about Antigone's burial of Polynices, Creon exclaims, 'While I'm alive,/no woman is going to lord it over me.'[15] From this statement, Creon expresses his fear that a woman could hold more power than he has himself. Additionally, Creon is angry not only because a woman has performed a forbidden act outside the *oikos*, but also because Antigone flaunts the act. According to Josine H. Blok, the '*oikos* ("household" and "family") was regarded as the proper space for free, respectable women. Considering that their domestic roles defined their lives, and they were expected to remain indoors, one would expect women's voices to be contained predominantly in situations inside the home.'[16] Therefore, Creon's anger towards Antigone's behaviour can also be explained by her performing a role that has not traditionally been assigned to her gender; by stepping outside her role into the political domain, she is taking on a masculine position. Indeed, in acting as she does – in assuming a kind of agency in the political realm – Antigone points to the gendered nature of the

---

[15] Sophocles, ll. 591-92, p86.

[16] Josine H. Blok, 'Women's Speech in Classical Athens', in *Making Silence Speak: Women's Voices in Greek Literature and Society,* ed. by André Lardinois and Laura McClure (Woodstock: Princeton University Press, 2001), pp95-106 (p100).

most quintessential elements of political life: as Nicole Loraux observes: 'the political process does not recognise a "citizenness", the language has no word for a woman from Athens'.[17] Thus, Creon responds to Antigone as though she were a man because there is no word to articulate her action of speaking outside of the *oikos* (household).

Furthermore, Creon is not the only character in the play to deem Antigone as manly; the Chorus also assume that Polynices' burial is carried out by a male: 'If you don't find the man who buried that corpse,/the very man, and produce him before my eyes [...].'[18] Commenting on Antigone's manliness, Judith Butler writes: 'Antigone comes, then, to act in ways that are called manly not only because she acts in defiance of the law but also because she assumes the voice of the law in committing the act against the law.'[19] Antigone, then, transforms from a female to a male by taking on the 'voice of the law'. However, Antigone faces consequences for this. By daring to speak as a female in a masculine forum, Antigone is sentenced to death by her uncle. She eventually takes her own life, and thus Antigone's voice is prematurely silenced.

---

[17]Nicole Loraux, 'Autochthony and the Athenian Imaginary', in *The Children of Athena*, trans. by Caroline Levine (Princeton: PUP, 1993), pp3-22 (p10)

[18]Sophocles, *Antigone*, ll. 346-7, p74.

[19]Judith Butler, 'Antigone's Claim', in *Antigone's Claim: Kinship between Life and Death* (New York: Columbia University Press, 2000), pp1-26 (p11).

Antigone, the Nature of the Law and the Debate Between the State and Individual

The Issue of Burial

Sophocles' *Antigone* revolves around the tragic issue of who is correct in the legislative interpretation of the law concerning Polynices' burial: state or individual? Antigone represents the position of the individual against the state, and Creon, who is also her uncle, stands for state authority. It is difficult to decide who is 'right' in this debate – or even if there is a 'right' answer. Antigone maintains that she has to bury Polynices despite Creon pronouncing him as a traitor, because of divine law. However, as will be explored in this section, Antigone's proclamation that she is following divine law is not necessarily as clear as it initially appears. You may like to think about who is 'right' in this debate, and how the debate of who is 'right' surfaces in Kamila Shamsie's *Home Fire*. Due to the sheer difficulty of the debate, scholars evidently disagree as to who would have been 'right' in this irresolvable debate.

Robert Garland, for instance, argues that Creon is correct to act as he does: 'So who is right [in the debate surrounding Polynices' burial]? Well, certainly Creon has precedent on his side. We have evidence from Athens dating to the turn of the fourth-century BCE that denial of burial was an established punishment for traitors, and there is no reason to doubt that such a law would have been in force long beforehand.'[20] Thus, from within the confines of the play, and from

---

[20]Robert Garland, 'Religion in *Antigone*', in *Looking at Antigone,* ed by David Stuttard (London: Bloomsbury, 2018), pp121-132 (p122).

a state-law perspective, it could be argued that Creon is simply following the rules established in fifth-century Athens; he is acting as a ruler should do, by following state-law. In this respect, the play is actively debating the law and power of democracy.

H.A. Shapiro agrees, writing that it is against the law of BCE fifth-century Athens to bury a traitor within the city walls. Shapiro suggests that Creon therefore is well within his rights to forbid the burial of Polynices.[21] Yet, Shapiro also admits that the struggle between the family and state arises here: as Polynices' kinsman, Creon should also be overseeing Polynices' burial. However, Creon does not give burial rites to Polynices until the end of the play, and only after his son and wife have both committed suicide. Opposed to the arguments for Creon forbidding the burial, Edward M. Harris is on Antigone's side. Harris explores how Athenians only forbade the burial of traitors in Attica; Creon, however, prohibited the burial completely. Therefore, Harris reasons that Antigone was within her rights to disobey Creon's order.[22]

Although it may seem from Harris' interpretation that Antigone was 'right' to bury Polynices, doubt can be cast on Antigone's motive for doing so. Scholars, such as Garland, reason that Antigone's act may not be noble: 'We may easily forgive Antigone for her desire to be graciously received by Hades, but there is another side to her behaviour that makes her much less attractive, namely her audacious claim that by burying her brother she is winning *kleos*.'[23] Typically

---

[21]H.A. Shapiro, 'The Wrath of Creon: Withholding Burial in Homer and Sophocles', *Helios*, 33 [Supplement] (2006), 119-34 (p120).

[22]Harris, p39.

[23]Garland, p124.

attributed to Athenian men, *kleos* is glory associated with an act. Antigone herself admits that even if she dies during the burial of her brother, 'that death will be a glory.'[24] Therefore, if Antigone's reason for burying her brother comes down to this, then not only does she become manly, but also she is using the divine law as a frame to hide her true intention of claiming *kleos*. In light of this, her claim becomes problematic as she is burying her brother not because of her duty to her family or divine law, but to win heroic glory.

Nevertheless, Antigone decides not to abide by state law and chooses to decide her own fate. She commits suicide, rather than enduring a living death and thus disrupts Creon's attempt to exercise power over her. Whatever her reasoning for prioritising her duty to her family over state law, her acts demonstrate she does not view state law as unbreakable or superior.

Antigone's Claim

Whilst being confronted by Creon about why she has buried her brother against the state's law, Antigone declares it is because of an unwritten divine law: 'Nor did I think your edict had such force/that you, a mere mortal, could override the gods/the great unshakeable traditions.'[25] Later in the play, however, questions are not just raised about the motives behind Antigone's burial of her brother, but also

---

[24]Sophocles, *Antigone*, ll. 86, p63.

[25]It is 'unwritten' in the sense that it is not physically written, in comparison, for instance to written law on stelae.

about her belief in divine law.[26] In comparison to Creon's arguably more concrete standpoint that he has obeyed state law, Antigone's position is less solid, as outlined by Tanja Staehler: '[Antigone] admits at certain points that there is no absolute guarantee of her interpreting the divine law correctly (even though she feels confident about her interpretation), and in that sense, she admits that she does not have unmediated or infallible access to the divine law.'[27] This reading becomes apparent when Antigone admits, 'It wasn't Zeus, not in the least/who made this proclamation – not to me'.[28] If it is not Zeus who made the proclamation to Antigone, is it Antigone herself who makes the law? Later in the play, Antigone gives reason to doubt that she definitively follows the law of the gods: 'Nor did that Justice, dwelling with the gods/beneath the earth, ordain such laws for men'.[29] This statement may unbalance Antigone's position that the law of the gods is higher in comparison to Creon's state law.

Furthermore, Antigone also appears to contradict what she has said about burying her brother because of her divine law, when she admits that she would have buried her brother anyway: 'Never, I tell you,/if I had been the mother of children/or if my husband died, exposed and rotting—/I'd never have taken this ordeal upon myself,

---

[26] For a seminal account of the complexity of the Greeks' relationship to the gods and their myths, see Paul Veyne, *Did the Greeks Believe Their Myths?* trans. by Paula Wissing (Chicago: The University of Chicago Press, 1988).

[27] Tanja Staehler, 'Antigone and the Nature of Law', in *Law and Philosophy*, ed. by Michael Freeman and Ross Harrison (Oxford University Press, 2007), pp137–56 (p141).

[28] Sophocles, *Antigone*, ll. 499-500, p82.

[29] Sophocles, *Antigone*, ll. 501-02, p82.

never defied our people's will.'[30] Antigone goes on to ask: 'What law, you ask, do I satisfy with what I say?'[31] In answer to this, Antigone gives the peculiar reasoning that she would not have committed the same act for either a husband or child as there would be the possibility of another.[32] For a brother, though, Antigone states this possibility is revoked as 'mother and father both lost in the halls of Death, /no brother could ever spring to light again.'[33]

Multiple reasons, as outlined above, seem to be favoured by Antigone for burying her brother. Thus, it is apparent that a clear answer cannot be gleaned from her reasoning.

Creon the Tyrant?

The complexity behind Antigone's burial of Polynices and her rationale for doing so, are also reflected in Creon's position. Creon's refusal to allow Antigone to bury her brother, and his lack of sympathy for Antigone's position, has led him to be deemed as tyrannical – especially since Antigone herself suggests that Creon is a tyrant: 'Luckily tyrants – the perquisites of power! /Ruthless power to do

---

[30] Sophocles, *Antigone*, ll. 995-999, p105.[3]

[1] Sophocles, *Antigone*, ll. 1000, p105.

[32] Interestingly, Antigone does have a child in Kamal Kann's *Aaliyah: After Antigone*. Performed in October 2021, the play ends with Aaliyah (Antigone) having a baby – named Antigone, who Aaliyah states is from an 'old Greek story' and 'stands up for what she believes in'. Fisher, *Aaliyah: After Antigone Review'*.

[33] Sophocles, *Antigone*, ll. 1003-04, p105.

and say what pleases *them*'.[34] Nancy J. Holland, too, echoes this common understanding of Creon: 'We all know who and what Creon was. He was a tyrant – a proto-Nazi, according to French playwright Jean Anouilh.'[35]

Other scholars suggest the opposite. Bonnie Honig reads Creon's character as non-tyrannical (a tyrannical leader is an oppressive leader), pointing out that Creon is acting within the context of fifth-century democratic principle. In this reading, Creon is not simply going against Antigone's wishes because he is tyrannous. Rather, he is performing his duty as a fifth-century leader in the interest of democracy: 'His [Creon's] ban on lamentation and his repeated emphasis on the harms of individuality represent the fifth-century democratic view.'[36] This interpretation may not align with contemporary readings of the play, but in light of a reading from the perspective of fifth-century Athens, Creon is well within his rights to exercise his power.

Misogyny is also another criticism Creon faces.[37] Contemporary scholars informed by feminist theory have highlighted the ways in which Creon's behaviour is misogynistic; for instance, he states: 'While I'm alive,/no woman is going to lord it over me.'[38] Whilst Creon is

---

[34] Sophocles, *Antigone*, ll. 566-7, p84.

[35] Holland, p1.

[36] Bonnie Honig, 'Mourning, membership, and the politics of exception: plotting Creon's conspiracy with democracy', in *Antigone, Interrupted* (New York: Cambridge University Press, 2013), pp95-120 (p98).

[37] The first chapter 'Antigone and Feminism: (Un)Silencing the Female Voice' explores Creon's misogynistic treatment of Antigone in more detail.

[38] Sophocles, *Antigone*, ll. 592-93, p86.

known for his misogynistic behaviour, this may not be his exclusive motive for treating Antigone as he does.

However, even if Creon is simply following fifth-century Athenian protocol, this does not automatically remove the misogynistic element and his disregard for family in his treatment of Antigone – and by extension Polynices – nor does it take into account the morality behind Antigone's actions. Failing also is Creon's ability to see that his niece is alienated in her position of wishing to bury her brother; he does not sympathise with her view until the end of the play, after Antigone has committed suicide.[39] Reasons for and against Creon's behaviour then exist, and just like in Antigone's case, a definitive conclusion cannot be reached on who is right or wrong.[40] The essence of this conflict is, ultimately, irresolvable.

SECTION TWO: KAMILA SHAMSIE'S *HOME FIRE*

Home Fire's Relationship to *Antigone*

We have now looked at Sophocles' *Antigone* in detail, and some of the themes that are key to the play, including gender, the nature of

---

[39] Aneeka does not commit suicide in *Home Fire*, but dies in a suicide bomber attack.

[40] Arguably, however, it could be said that Creon is proven 'wrong', when his wife and son commit suicide at the end of the play.

the law and the debate between the state and the individual. Now, we shall turn to look at Kamila Shamsie's *Home Fire* and how gender, the nature of the law and the debate between the state and the individual are presented in Shamsie's novel. Although we will think about the relationship between the ancient play and the novel, you may like to think now about how the connections emerge between *Antigone* and *Home Fire,* and how they differ.

In Shamsie's tale, as there is only one brother, Parvaiz, there is no conflict between two brothers. There are, however, two sisters: Aneeka plays the part of Antigone, and Isma, Ismene. The brother, Parvaiz, is based on Polynices. Although the novel shifts perspectives from character to character, a large proportion of *Home Fire* concentrates on how a family is torn apart by a brother's betrayal. Shamsie's rewriting of the tale from a British Muslim perspective not only speaks to key political and ethical issues of our age but gives voice to viewpoints seldom listened to in contemporary Britain.[41] Sisters Aneeka (Antigone, the younger) and Isma (Ismene, the older) and their brother Parvaiz (Polynices) are put at the heart of the novel, in opposition to Karamat (Creon) and his son Eamonn (Haemon).[42]

Speaking about the elements of the *Antigone* that Shamsie alters, Natalie Haynes states how:

---

[41] Lau and Mendes outline how British Muslims are seldom listened to as a result of the following view: 'Muslim immigrants [are seen] as a threat to Western "achievements" in terms of gender equality and freedom of speech. Widely covered by the media and increasingly adopted by mainstream political parties, including social democrats, this populist far-right rhetoric is now part of the new common sense, filling up the space of the failed social-democratic economic promises of the post-war period in Europe and the US.' Lau and Mendes, p54.

[42] Eamonn is a complicated character, who is in both cahoots with the family, as well as opposition.

It is in this move away from the earliest incarnations of the myth that Shamsie's novel is most successful: she drops the incestuous nature of the children's parentage, and ditches the second brother, so that Parvaiz is guilty of all kinds of things, but not fratricide.[43]

Removing prominent features of Sophocles' *Antigone*, such as the incestuous parentage, updates *Antigone*, and brings it careering into the twenty-first century. In a review of *Home Fire*, Jason Steger observes that '*Home Fire* [...] is bang up to date even if it is a reimagining of Sophocles' *Antigone* and tackles similar issues such as the obligations of the citizen in the face of state injustice and the importance of natural law compared with that of man-made law.'[44]

The removal of citizenship is one of the key themes of *Home Fire*, which will be explored in this study guide. Although Antigone does not have her citizenship removed in Sophocles' play, a similarity can be drawn between Antigone and Parvaiz. Antigone is an outcast because she has broken state law and is sentenced to death. Parvaiz is an outcast, as by going to Syria, he is deemed to be a terrorist by the British state. Karamat, who is a non-practicing British Muslim, then decides to remove Parvaiz's British citizenship after Parvaiz's death so he cannot be buried in Britain. We may like to think about how Shamsie's *Home Fire* bears a relationship to the removal of Shamima Begum's citizenship, a case which as you may remember, appears in the news:

---

[43] Natalie Haynes, '*Home Fire* by Kamila Shamsie review – a contemporary reworking of Sophocles' *The Guardian*, 10 August 2017, Section Books

[44] Jason Steger, 'Kamila Shamsie-Interview', *The Age Australia*, 10 February 2018

'Former Home Secretary Sajid Javid stripped her [Shamima Begum] of her UK citizenship later that month. A tribunal ruled that Ms Begum could be stripped of her nationality because she had not been left stateless. The Special Immigration Appeals Commission (SIAC), a semi-secret court which hears national security cases, said she could instead turn to Bangladesh for citizenship.'[45]

At the time Shamsie wrote *Home Fire*, Shamima Begum had not had her citizenship removed. However, you would like to think about Shamima Begum's case and the prominence of this for why Kamila Shamsie has chosen to resurrect an ancient story in a modern setting.

In the next part of this study guide, we will examine the portrayal of gender relations in *Home Fire*, before moving on to look at the nature of the law and the removal of Parvaiz's citizenship.

Home Fire and Gender Relations

In Kamila Shamsie's *Home Fire*, like Sophocles' *Antigone*, the female voice is also silenced by a male authority. Aneeka, the Antigone-based character, requests to return her brother Parvaiz back to England. However, this is against the wishes of state-leader Karamat. Both Karamat, and his son Eamonn demonstrate misogynistic attitudes, as well as Islamophobia, towards women throughout the novel. This sentiment is echoed by the media also, who are shown to mirror

---

[45]'Shamima Begum loses first stage of appeal over Citizenship', *BBC News* <https://www.bbc.co.uk/news/uk-51413040>, 7 February 2020 [accessed 13.01.21].

Eamonn and Karamat's deeply troubling behaviour towards Muslim women: 'IS THIS THE FACE OF EVIL?' a tabloid asked, illustrating the question with a picture of the girl howling as dust flew around her. Slag, terrorist-spawn, enemy-of-Britain.'[46]

Comparing Sophocles' *Antigone* to Shamsie's *Home Fire*, Lisa Lau and Ana Cristina Mendes outline, 'Because of the action of a male family member, Sophocles' and Shamsie's Antigones decide they must step out of the privacy of home spaces into public arenas to challenge authorities and embroil themselves in protests which are not only deeply personal, but political.'[47] Both Antigones share the commonality that their individual political actions are suppressed by a male authority figure. A similarity is also shared by both women that they are consequently reduced to a child-like state by a male for speaking out.

Karamat's son and Aneeka's lover Eamonn expresses a misogynistic attitude similar to his father. Whilst Eamonn does eventually show his commitment to Aneeka – they are implied to die together at the end of the novel – this does not rule out Eamonn's potentially missogynistic.

Within an early encounter with Isma and Eamonn in the novel the reader learns of Eamonn's troubled relationship with religion, symbolised by Aneeka's hijab. When in a relationship with Aneeka, Eamonn questions her need to wear the hijab: '"Why'd you have to do that?" he said, and she brushed the end of the scarf against his

---

[46] 'Shamsie, p299.

[47] Lisa Lau and Ana Cristina Mendes, 'Twenty-First-Century Antigones: The Postcolonial Woman Shaped by 9/11 in Kamila Shamsie's Home Fire', *Studies in the Novel*, 53.1 (2021), 54–68 (pp54-55).

throat and said "I get to choose which part of me I want strangers to look at, and which are for you."⁴⁸ Rehana Ahmed writes that Eamonn's misunderstanding of Aneeka is troubling because: 'Despite Eamonn's part-Muslim heritage (he is of Pakistani and white Irish American descent), his gaze is clearly exoticising, at times reducing Aneeka to the double-sided Orientalist stereotype of the veiled Muslim woman as chaste yet lascivious, inaccessible yet promiscuous, mysterious yet the ultimate object of knowledge. In a series of images, her religiosity, emblematised by her hijab, overlays her sexualised body.'⁴⁹

Karamat, Eamonn's father also demonstrates an Islamophobic attitude, and sexualises Aneeka in a comparably problematic way. Questioning his son, Eamonn, about his relationship with Aneeka, Karamat asks Eamonn whether Aneeka's religion prevents her from having sex, making a crude gesture in the process: '"Uh huh. But she has no problem –" He brought the palms of his hands together and then separated them.'⁵⁰ Reflecting on Eamonn's decision to enter a relationship with Aneeka later on in the novel, Karamat maintains that 'Aneeka Pasha was the kind of girl who would do anything. [...] His poor boy never stood a chance.'⁵¹ Karamat recognises that Aneeka's ability to 'do anything' translates into having a political ability, which is ultimately silenced because of Karamat's misogyny.

---

⁴⁸Shamsie, pp71-72.

⁴⁹Rehana Ahmed, 'Towards an Ethics of Reading Muslims: Encountering Difference in Kamila Shamsie's *Home Fire*', *Textual Practice*, 35.7 (2021), 1145–61 (p1149).

⁵⁰Shamsie, p106.

⁵¹Shamsie, p226.

Karamat is thus guilty of the same crime as Hegel. From Karamat's point of view, Eamonn, and by extension Creon, are not to blame for the political actions that have been undertaken – the blame ultimately rests with the female.

When it comes to commenting on Aneeka's political actions, at first, it appears that Karamat is, surprisingly, stunned. Receiving a television broadcast of Aneeka in the park with the corpse of her brother, Karamat utters the word: 'Impressive.'[52] Yet, this opinion quickly changes. Mirroring Creon – who treats Antigone as a child, because she is a woman who acts outside of the *oikos* – Karamat treats Aneeka in a similar way for her political actions.[53]

Attempting to display his Britishness – and Aneeka's inability to be British – Karamat, 'spun the paperweight, watched the unicorn and lion animate, smiled. After all the noise and spectacle, she was just a silly girl.' Lions and unicorns are images associated with Britishness, tools for Karamat's guise as a British citizen. From this gesture, it is evident that Karamat's acts are performative, in order to appear like a 'real' British citizen. Under this act, Karamat infantilises Aneeka's political actions. He does not really listen to the words that she is saying. Karamat thus silences her political voice, not only as she is a woman, but also because she is a Muslim. Hence, the perspective of the British Muslim that Shamsie has sought to amplify throughout the novel is silenced by the male political leader who, by referring her to as a 'little girl', views Aneeka's actions as child-like.

---

[52]Shamsie, p224.

[53]Shamsie, p225.

The Nature of the Law in *Home Fire*

Focussing on the portrayal of the nature of law in Kamila Shamsie's *Home Fire*, this part of the study guide will revive the age-old debate of state law versus the individual in *Antigone* from a British Muslim's perspective. We shall concentrate on Parvaiz's loss of citizenship and how Aneeka, a practicing Muslim, struggles to reclaim it, against state-ruler Karamat, the Creon based character and a non-practicing Muslim.

Revolving around the issue of Parvaiz's citizenship are different readings of the law and policy. The play's transformation into a novel allows for further exploration of how the law should be interpreted, and the moral implications beyond these decisions. The two sisters provide an example of the difficulties of interpreting the law, and also how claims between the state and individual often struggle to be separated. Similar to Sophocles' characters, Isma and Aneeka are presented in a complicated sororal relationship: sisters that both love each other and clash.[54] Our memories of Sophocles' *Antigone* somehow seem to link the way we shape our expectations of how Antigone should behave in subsequent adaptations.[55] Like Sophocles' Ismene, the oldest sister, Isma, in *Home Fire* is presented as the sensible, caring sibling who has taken on the role of parent. The siblings and their father, it is revealed later, had been taken to

---

[54] See the second chapter 'Antigone and Sisterhood' for more on the sister-sister relationship, including a reading of the sister-sister relationship where this interpretation is questioned.

[55] The story of the *Antigone* thus surfaces as the vehicle through which this conflict is presented, but the sister's interpretation of the law, although bearing similarities to the Theban play, also differs in Shamsie's narrative.

Guantanamo prison, where it is presumed that he had died. Shaping her personality, these events ultimately lead Isma to be more levelheaded than her younger sister, Aneeka, but also separates the two sisters further.

Whilst the two sisters are presented as caring for each other at moments in the novel, the issue that really divides them is their brother Parvaiz. Like Antigone, Aneeka's obsession with the brother-sister relationship leads to untimely deaths.[56] Shortly after arriving in America to begin her PhD, Isma logs online to speak to her sister, Aneeka and discovers that Parvaiz, who has gone to Syria, is online:

> [There] had only been one time she had truly, purely missed her brother without adjectives such as "ungrateful" and "selfish" slicing through the feeling of loss. Now she looked at his name on the screen, her mouth forming prayers to keep Aneeka from logging on, the adjectives forming thick in her mind. Aneeka must learn to think of him as lost for ever.[57]

In Isma's narrative, the complex relationship that Isma has with her brother, Parvaiz, and the struggles of their relationship are revealed. On the one hand, as a sister, Isma truly loves her brother. But on the other hand, Isma feels betrayed that Parvaiz has gone to Syria: she believes he is selfish for not thinking about the implications this may cause for the two sisters, as Muslims. This issue is further complicated

---

[56] Whilst we actually witness Parvaiz's death, Aneeka's death is not fully confirmed as we do not witness it at the end of the novel. Merely, Aneeka's 'death' is implied death; the novel actually ends in a lover's embrace, before what we anticipate is death caused by the impending bomb: 'For a moment they are two lovers in a park, under an ancient tree, sun-dappled, beautiful and at peace.' Shamsie, p260.

[57] Shamsie, p12.

when Isma, like Ismene in Sophocles' *Antigone*, wants to protect her sister from the consequences of state law, but feels an obligation to her family. In order to do this, it is revealed that Isma had told the British police about Parvaiz to protect herself, but ultimately, to protect Aneeka. Family and state law again become entangled. The clash of views that the sisters share means that Aneeka is alone – at least for most of the novel – with how she feels about her brother.

Later on, Aneeka discovers that it was Isma who had told the police about their brother, and Aneeka cannot understand why Isma would take the side of the state law. Isma tells Aneeka that as British Muslims, they are 'in no position to let the state question our loyalties'.[58] In Sophocles' *Antigone,* Ismene states that the sisters have to obey the law because they are women: 'Remember we are women,/we're not born to contend with men.'[59] Shamsie, however, supercharges Muslim identity with law. If a British Muslim were to break state law, the consequences could result in them being labelled terrorists.

Further on in the novel, when Parvaiz dies, Isma simply states to Aneeka: 'Go back to uni, study the law. Accept the law, even when it's unjust.'[60] For Isma, then, the state law must be abided by at all costs, even in the event of the death of their brother. However, like Sophocles' Antigone, Aneeka refuses to accept state law and goes beyond it to retrieve their brother's corpse. Complicating Aneeka's interpretation of the law even further is that she is a student at university. This suggests that in her study of the state law – potentially

---

[58]Shamsie, p42.

[59]Sophocles, *Antigone,* ll. 74-75, p62.

[60]Shamsie, p196.

having the future of a lawyer – she should be an advocate for upholding the state law.[61] Yet, as demonstrated by her determination to retrieve her brother's corpse, this is far from the case.

Aneeka is not the only one who questions state law, however. Despite Isma's appearance, like Sophocles' Ismene as an upholder of state-law, there are points in the novel when Isma questions state law, just like her sister Aneeka. During a university lecture, Isma uses her voice to illustrate the position faced by the British Muslim:

> *Would you like to say something Ms Pasha?* "Yes, Dr Shah, if you look at colonial laws you'll see plenty of precedent for depriving people of their rights; the only difference is that this time it's being applied to British citizens, and even that's not as much of a change as you might think, because they're rhetorically being made unBritish." *Say more.* "The 7/7 terrorists were never described by the media as "British terrorist." "Even when the word "British" was used it was always "British of Pakistani descent" or "British Muslim" or, my favourite, "British passport-holders", always something interposed between their Britishness and terrorism." *Well you have quite a voice when you decide to use it.*[62]

This passage clearly highlights the moral implications for the application of state law and points out it is not always necessarily 'right'. Ironically, it is a speech which anticipates how Aneeka and (eventually) Isma will challenge state law when it is applied to their brother. Demonstrating that state law can easily be overturned, the lecturer pre-empts that both Aneeka and Isma are able to use their

---

[61] During a conversation towards the beginning of the novel, Aneeka rebukes Isma for reporting their brother Parvaiz to the police. See pp41-42 of *Home Fire* for this conversation between the two sisters.

[62] Shamsie, p38.

voices to question state law when it is being utilised in a way that does not necessarily benefit the citizen. Above, Isma outlines how state law has been utilised in a racist way, particularly, in the case of British Muslims. Occurring quite early in the novel, Isma's speech foreshadows how Aneeka will question the state law, to bring her brother home, in her own interpretation of justice. This is a factor that further distances Aneeka from not only her family, but also her British identity.

Aneeka seeks her own justice, beyond state law, upon Parvaiz's death, and resolves to retrieve his body. This moment is cemented during an encounter with Isma, from which the fraught relationship between the two is fractured further. Aneeka becomes distant from her sister, due to their conflicting beliefs. Aneeka rebukes any attempt that Isma makes to repair their relationship, believing that Isma betrayed Parvaiz. Pleading with her sister, Isma states: 'That [the betrayal] has nothing to do with why he's dead. You have to forgive me.'[63]

Subsequently, religion is brought into the discussion around Parvaiz's death. Whilst Isma believes in heaven and hell as parables, Aneeka decides to bring Parvaiz home; in the name of what she is not sure: 'I don't know the things you know. Life, death, heaven, hell, god soul. I only know Parvaiz.'[64] Although Aneeka is not certain what has happened to Parvaiz after his death, she knows that she must bring him home. This line is arguably a direct allusion to Antigone's line: 'Never, I tell you,/if I had been the mother of children/

---

[63]Shamsie, p195.

[64]Shamsie, p196.

or if my husband died, exposed and rotting—/I'd never have taken this ordeal upon myself, never defied our people's will.'[65] This line is uttered by Antigone just before she goes to her death. Antigone's words here seem to indicate that she has not buried her brother because of divine law, despite stating otherwise earlier in the play.[66]

Disagreeing with Aneeka, Isma tries to persuade her otherwise. Aneeka, like Antigone, refuses to listen to Isma, exclaiming: 'You don't love either justice or our brother if you can say that.'[67] Whilst Isma remains firmly on the side of state law (although she changes her mind later on in the novel), Aneeka opposes it and creates her own unique claim to the law. In the case of the marginalised voice of the British Muslim, this is essential to help amplify their voice.[68] The fact that Isma changes her mind as to which law to support, shows the flexible and unreliable nature of the law. A link can again be drawn to the flexible nature of the *Antigone* story, in that Aneeka, like Antigone, makes her individual claim against the state. Whilst Antigone spoke from Thebes, Aneeka speaks thousands of years later from the viewpoint of a minority perspective.

Therefore, both Aneeka and Isma interpret justice differently,

---

[65] Sophocles, *Antigone,* ll. 995-999, p105.

[66] See the chapter's first section for discussion about this issue.

[67] Shamsie, p196.

[68] The issue of citizenship is also explored further in *Aaliyah: After Antigone,* by Kamal Kann. Performed in Bradford, October 2021, the brother Syed (Polynices) is threatened with deportation back to Bangladesh. Aaliyah (Antigone) wishes to save her brother from this fate, as Syed is gay, and homosexuality is illegal in Bangladesh. Syed's actions are compared by the Prime Minister, on Zoom, to that of Covid-19; in other words, being a Muslim (terrorist) is a virus. Fisher, '*Aaliyah: After Antigone* Review'.

demonstrating the slippery nature of the law, as a human, not necessarily a divine, construct. Within these different interpretations of the law, Aneeka also becomes further cut-off from her family, as she is almost solely alone in her decision to bury her brother.

The Issue of Citizenship in *Home Fire*

Karamat makes the decision to remove Parvaiz's citizenship, which drives Aneeka even further in her determination to pursue individual law to bring her brother home.[69] The narratives of the conflict in both Sophocles' *Antigone* and Kamila Shamsie's *Home Fire* sometimes share surprising similarities. Like Antigone – who is in the realm of the living dead when Creon strips her of her rights – Parvaiz's citizenship is stripped whilst he is dead:

> "'And Pervys Pasha was a dual national?' 'That's correct. Of Britain and Pakistan.' 'Practically speaking, does this have any consequences now he's dead?' 'His body will be repatriated to his home nation, Pakistan.'"[70]

Parvaiz's citizenship status is complicated by his dual nationality but also allows him to claim citizenship in two nations, Britain and Pakistan. The return of Parvaiz's body to Pakistan, effectively removes his British citizenship. Karamat comments how his predecessor did not exercise their powers harshly enough in cases to remove

---

[69] Shamsie, p188.
[70] Shamsie, p188.

citizenship.[71] Instead, Karamat goes further than his predecessor, and uses his political position to remove Parvaiz's British citizenship, stating that the law should 'determine someone's fitness for citizenship based on their actions, not on accidents of birth.'[72] Karamat's extreme view implies that someone's actions – which could be based on problematic criteria – should determine their citizenship, not 'accidents' of birth. By stating this, Karamat implies that despite Parvaiz's birth in the UK, he is still not effectively British.[73] Additionally, the impact of the power Karamat exercises extends wider than just Parvaiz. Applied to those who are British and Muslim, Karamat is effectively saying that these people are not British because they identify as Muslim.

Whilst both Aneeka and Isma differ in their interpretations of justice, Karamat does not waver in his execution of the law until the end of the story, as is the case with Creon. Based on Sophocles' Creon, in *Home Fire*, Karamat becomes Home Secretary, the first British Muslim to do so (in the novel). The obvious claim that narratives of the tragic conflict are non-universal, are hereby demonstrated by the differing backgrounds of those that represent the state positions: Creon

---

[71]Shamsie, p214.

[72]Providing a similar question into what would happen if Antigone's brother Polynices had been a slave, Tina Chanter refers to Edith Hall, who asks how his corpse would have been treated given his slave status: 'Given Creon's efforts to reduce Polynices to nothing but a traitor, and therefore in some senses "worse" than a barbarian/slave, the status of Polynices' humanity is very much at stake in Antigone's burial of his corpse.' Chanter, pxxi.

[73]Karamat's ability to change from a realist to moralist position at the end of the novel is similar to Isma's case. It also further demonstrates how these positions fail to be indistinguishable.

is from Thebes, Karamat from a British Muslim background. Yet, the ambivalence of whether those that represent state authorities are 'right' in the dispute are presented through the character of Karamat, and likewise Creon, through the vehicle of the *Antigone* story.[74]

An unlikely candidate for Home Secretary, Karamat's own relationship to Islam is complicated, and overall, he feels alienated from his Muslim identity. On that basis, Karamat is (or was) a practising Muslim, but he also does everything he can to get away from being identified as such for political gain. Again, the confusion of religion and politics surfaces. Creon in Sophocles' *Antigone* first appears to act as the state, but he also has gods on his side: 'My countrymen,/the ship of the state is safe./The gods who rocker,/after a long, merciless pounding in the storm,/have righted her once more.'[75] Creon also states that 'Zeus [is] my witness.'[76] Thus, the distinction that, for example, Hegel draws between the realms is never fully clear. Here, Shamsie reflects this with Karamat's complex relationship to Islam in her 'updating' of the terms of *Antigone*.

Complicating Karamat's position further, Karamat's son, Eamonn, has a relationship with Aneeka, thus the state and individual again become tangled. As the reader, we know that Aneeka and Eamonn's relationship is double-edged, as Aneeka originally forms a relationship with Eamonn for political gain, to bring her brother home, in opposition to Karamat's political views. In Sophocles' *Antigone*,

---

[74]See earlier in this chapter for reasons for and against Creon being right.
[75]Sophocles, *Antigone*, ll. 180-82, p67.
[76]Sophocles, *Antigone*, ll. 205, p67.

Creon's son, Haemon, is Antigone's fiancé. Eventually, Eamonn, like Antigone's Haemon, does become Aneeka's fiancé. Whilst Eamonn resembles Sophocles' Haemon in many ways, Eamonn's name has Irish roots. Isma comments that Eamonn's name is 'an Irish spelling to disguise a Muslim name – Ayman became Eamonn so that people would know the father had integrated'.[77] Respelling the name to disguise the Muslim heritage is so that Eamonn can appear more 'British'. Yet, the Irish name chosen may carry further intriguing significance. Karamat's wife is from Ireland, a nation with a long experience of British colonialism, of challenges to identity and the imposing of external laws. In light of the political context of *Home Fire*, the discussion of state versus the individual and Eamonn's name, recent Irish history may be recalled in the form of the IRA and The Troubles.

Executing state power, and ignoring the protests of those around him, Karamat, like Creon, acts. In Sophocles' *Antigone*, Creon protests, 'The city is the king's – that's the law!'[78] Speaking like this, it is clear that Creon believes that the city is his – and his alone – and this line could help formulate the interpretation that he is a tyrant. Arguing for a more democratic perspective, Haemon insists that 'it is no city at all, owned by one man alone.'[79] Mirroring Sophocles' *Antigone*, Shamsie's *Home Fire* also hosts a similar conversation between man and son. Eamonn tries to get Karamat to see the flaws in his power, and also reminds him of the high political stake of

---

[77] Shamsie, pp15-16.

[78] Sophocles, *Antigone*, l. 825, p97.

[79] Sophocles, *Antigone*, l. 824, p97.

Parvaiz's situation: 'A government that sends its citizens to some other country when they act in ways they don't like. Doesn't that say we can't deal with our own problems?'[80] Continuing to plead with his father, Eamonn tries to make Karamat see Aneeka's perspective: 'And stopping a family from burying its own – that never looks good. That's what people are beginning to say around me. If your advisers won't tell you this, your son will.'[81] Regardless of his son's protests, big-headed Karamat, similarly to Creon, ignores his son, exclaiming: '"My son, schooling me in politics from his vantage point among landed gentry.'[82] Therefore, Karamat reflects Creon. Karamat only rethinks his actions when it is too late, when both son and Aneeka are dead.[83]

Notwithstanding reader's likely expectations that the novel will reflect Sophocles' *Antigone* and the tragedy of the unresolved conflict therein, that is also the case with *Home Fire*. Believing that those who have been deemed as terrorists are not worthy of citizenship, Karamat declares that Parvaiz's body cannot be returned to British soil. Aneeka refuses to listen, and travels to Pakistan to retrieve her brother's body – despite Karamat's attempt to stop her individual claim to the law. Overall, the novel demonstrates the nature of its tragedy in the inability to reach a definitive conclusion and fully separate the two sides in the struggle between family and state.

---

[80]Shamsie, pp217-18.

[81]Shamsie, p218.

[82]Shamsie, p218.

[83]Although it could be said that Creon's actions towards Antigone are more problematic, given that Antigone is Creon's niece – and he upholds the state law above the familial, until his son's and wife's deaths.

Concluding Thoughts

This study has considered the relationship between *Antigone* and *Home Fire,* looking at issues of gender, the nature of the law and the citizenship. This conclusion will turn to look at some of the reasons why Shamsie's novel, like Sophocles' *Antigone* will not be forgotten; whilst *Antigone* has been returned to time and time again and thus has stood the test of time, there is also reason why Shamsie's adaptation of the ancient play has its own merits and will be returned to as time passes.

Firstly, however, there is reason to consider how without *Antigone, Home Fire* may have never been the novel that we know by now. Speaking about *Antigone,* Sam McBean outlines the feminist critic's refusal to leave Antigone in the past:

> Temporal drag provides a means of considering Antigone as a practice that disrupts any concept of cohesive feminist historical narratives of progress. The frequent backwards iterations of Antigone in feminism refuse to leave her be, to properly bury her, and instead, through consistently bringing her into various presents, insist on keeping the past a contested ground.[84]

Whilst other myths have also been returned to, Antigone's repeated occurrence in both critical attention and the contemporary novel seem to heavily outweigh the focus on other myths. Refusing to 'properly bury' Antigone, therefore, suggests that there is a fascination with Antigone that causes her to be continuously at the centre of many critical interpretations. Much of this is due to the unresolved

---

[84]Sam McBean, 'Dragging the not-yet', in *Feminism's Queer Temporalities* (Oxon: Routledge, 2016), pp 27-48 (p28).

tensions that charge the play, and which continue to be revisited in contemporary adaptation, such as *Home Fire* and Joydeep Roy-Bhattacharya's *The Watch*.

The popularity of Antigone, then, as McBean highlights above could definitely be said to have influenced Shamsie's decision to base her novel on Sophocles' play. In an interview, Shamsie speaks about her decision to base her novel on the play:

> The idea started because a theater director asked me to think about re-writing the Ancient Greek play *Antigone* in a contemporary British context. When I read the play – which has at its center two sisters who respond differently to the legal repercussions of their brother's act of treason – I knew immediately that I wanted to connect it to a story that was very much in the news at the time, that of young British Muslims and their relationship with the British state. I didn't end up writing it as a play; I'm a novelist, so that's the form I wanted to use to tell the story.[85]

Can Shamsie's *Home Fire*, then be a novel on its own terms? Do you need to have read *Antigone* to understand *Home Fire*? It would seem from the excerpt in Shamsie's interview that you would need to have a thorough understanding of the *Antigone* before you read *Home Fire*. Yet, I would argue that although it is of course extremely helpful – as this book has outlined – to have knowledge about Sophocles' play before reading *Home Fire*, it is not necessarily essential to have knowledge about *Antigone* before reading *Home Fire*.

One reason for this is an obvious one: *Home Fire* has been written in the form of the novel and importantly is more accessible than the

---

[85] https://www.thejakartapost.com/life/2018/04/04/interview-kamila-shamsie-talks-about-home-fire-minorities-and-terrorism.html

ancient play written or performed in Ancient Greek. *Home Fire* has been written in English: you do not need to have gone to university to study Classics or have learnt Ancient Greek to consume the tale. The way in which we consume the tale has also changed. Sophocles wrote *Antigone* with the intention of it being watched by an audience in an Ancient Greek theatre. Thousands of years later, *Antigone* does of course continue to dazzle audiences. In the present time, however, *Antigone* will not just be performed on stage. We are now able to read and listen to audiobooks of novels, and also watch recordings and livestreams of the performance of *Antigone* adaptations. This means that the flexibility of how we consume *Antigone* has changed; we are not limited to having to go a theatre and interrupt our busy lives – *Antigone* can be consumed anywhere, at any time.

Although these reasons are of course important, perhaps the most important reason for the recurrence of *Home Fire* in the future over other adaptations of *Antigone* are the issues that the novels covers and the way that Shamsie brings the adaptation hurtling into the twenty first century. Part of the attractiveness of *Antigone* is the way in which the issues that the play covers remain as important today as when they were first written. The crucial factor in adapting *Antigone* is making it relatable. In the current historical moment, the issues that *Home Fire* covers are extremely important, but also relatable to the present day. Shamsie's addition of setting the *Antigone* story in a British Muslim context continues to add to its merits. Islamophobia, the threat of terror and what it means to be 'British' are questions that will continue to echo for years to come. Not only does the novel provide a window into the lives of British Muslims, but issues questions of family loyalty and identity – Parvaiz's struggle with his sisters, and the search for a father figure – are aspects that all human beings can relate to. Thus, this means that Shamsie's tale set in the contemporary moment is as timeless as Sophocles' *Antigone*.